Spotlight on Colorado

COLORADO'S CHANGING CITIES

Then and Now

Sarah Machajewski

PowerKiDS press™

NEW YORK

Published in 2016 by The Rosen Publishing Group, Inc.
29 East 21st Street, New York, NY 10010

Book Design: Iron Cupcake Design

Cataloging-in-Publication Data

Names: Machajewski, Sarah.
Title: Colorado's changing cities / Sarah Machajewski.
Description: New York : PowerKids Press, 2016. | Series: Spotlight on Colorado | Includes index.
Identifiers: ISBN 9781499414974 (pbk.) | ISBN 9781499414998 (6 pack) | ISBN 9781499415025 (library bound)
Subjects: LCSH: Colorado--Juvenile literature. | Cities and towns--Growth--Juvenile literature. | City planning--Juvenile literature.
Classification: LCC F776.3 M28 2016 | DDC 978.8--dc23

Photo Credits: LOT 13923, no. 197/loc.gov, cover; welcomia/Shutterstock.com, 3; f11photo/Shutterstock.com, 5; pavalena/Shutterstock.com, 6; Dennis Adams, Federal Highway Administration; color-corrected by Howcheng/ http://www.fhwa.dot.gov/byways/photos/51351/File:DowntownLeadvilleCO.jpg/Wikimedia Commons, 7; LC-DIG-ppmsca-09570/loc.gov, 9; Hulton Archive/Getty Images, 10; LC-D418-2550/loc.gov, 11; Everett Historical/Shutterstock.com, 12; Henryk Sadura/Shutterstock.com, 13; f11photo/Shutterstock.com, 15; Mark Hayes/Shutterstock.com, 17; Albert Pego/Shutterstock.com, 19; Robert27/Shutterstock.com, 21; welcomia/Shutterstock.com, 22; saraporn/Shutterstock.com, 23; AP Photo/Nathan Bilow, 24; AP Photo/Mickey Krakowski, 25; hecke61/Shutterstock.com, 26; Janis Maleckis/Shutterstock.com, 27; Brady-Handy Photograph Collection (Library of Congress)./File:Sherman, John.jpg/Wikimedia Commons, 27; Erik Patton/Shutterstock.com, 28; Denim Pete/Shutterstock.com, 29; AP Photo/The Denver Post, 30; AP Photo/The Denver Post, 31; Topical Press Agency/Getty Images, 33; Stocksnapper/Shutterstock.com, 34; Phillip Rubino/Shutterstock.com, 35; Christopher Tomlinson/The Grand Junction Daily Sentinel via AP, 36; AP PHOTO/DAILY SENTINEL, Christopher Tomlinson, 36; Zack Frank/Shutterstock.com, 37; John Hoffman/Shutterstock.com, 38; RyFlip/Shutterstock.com, 39; Jaminnbenji/Shutterstock.com, 40; John Hoffman/Shutterstock.com, 41; Mr. Klein/Shutterstock.com, 42; Fredlyfish4/Shutterstock.com, 43; Arina P Habich/Shutterstock.com, 44.

Manufactured in the United States of America

Contents

CHAPTER 1

The Great State of Colorado

When somebody talks about Colorado, what do you picture? For many people, just the mention of the state's name brings to mind the towering Rocky Mountains. Maybe you think of the ancient red rock formations that dot the state. Other people may imagine the wide, open land where cattle and other livestock roam. These natural features are home to bears, moose, elk, mountain lions, and more. There are pine trees as tall as the sky and plains as far as the eye can see.

Sure, Colorado is known for its beautiful natural landscapes. But there's more to the state than just that. Colorado has a cultural landscape, too. It comes from the 271 cities that lie within its borders. Each city has a **unique** identity, which was created by its colorful past and is shaped by its interesting present. Some

COLORADO'S OLDEST CITY

Hispanic families from New Mexico formed San Luis, Colorado, in 1851. These early pioneers migrated to the southeast corner of the state to establish settlements under land grants that were given by the governor of Santa Fe, which was at the time under Mexican rule. They created the first permanent settlement in Colorado. Today, it's the state's oldest continuously occupied town and the site of Colorado's oldest church.

Civic Center Park is located in the middle of the bustling, metropolitan city of Denver.

of these cities are a "mile high," while others are **boomtowns** that went bust.

Colorado's cities have changed a lot since the first one was founded in 1851. They've transformed from simple mining or railroad towns into **metropolitan** cities that are on the cutting edge of art, research, and urban development. Today, we study Colorado's changing cities to learn more about the Rocky Mountain state.

A boomtown is a city that grows rapidly because of something important that's happened, such as the discovery of gold or oil nearby. Many Colorado cities began as boomtowns.

CHAPTER 2

Colorado's Urban Places

Colorado is a wide, square-shaped state. It covers 104,094 square miles (269,602 sq km). It's bordered by Wyoming, Nebraska, Kansas, Oklahoma, New Mexico, Arizona, and Utah.

There are 271 incorporated municipalities in Colorado. An incorporated municipality

At 226 miles (374 km), the Front Range Urban Corridor runs from Cheyenne, Wyoming, through Denver, to Pueblo, Colorado.

The majority of Coloradans live in the Front Range Urban Corridor, but there are cities across the state of Colorado.

Denver is the most populated city in Colorado.

is a county, city, or town that has its own government. Local governments can make their own laws. However, they have to follow the laws set by the state government.

Of the 271 municipalities in Colorado, there are 196 towns and 73 cities. Colorado is unique because it has two places that are considered to be both a city *and* a county. These two places are Denver and Broomfield.

When you look at a map, it's easy to see how Colorado's geography has influenced where cities are located. In most places, cities are spread throughout the state. Most of Colorado's cities, however, lie in a corridor that runs from north to south. This corridor is on the eastern face of the Rocky Mountains, where the plains and mountains meet. It's called the Front Range Urban Corridor. Almost 85 percent of Colorado's population lives there. Once you pass through this range, the rest of the state is rural and mountainous. Long ago (and even today), it must've been easier to settle in and travel through the flat Front Range than it would've been to tame the mountain geography.

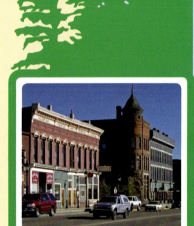

THE TWO-MILE-HIGH CITY

Leadville, Colorado, is the highest incorporated city in the United States. It sits at an elevation of 10,152 feet (3,094 m)!

CHAPTER 3

The History of Denver

Denver may be the best-known city in Colorado, and it's also one that has experienced great change. Arapaho Indians occupied the land long before the city was settled. They used it as a stopover while they traveled during hunts and often camped there in large numbers. Native Americans in Colorado first came into contact with white settlers through the traders and fur trappers who traveled through their land. Then, in 1858, everything changed.

A group of **prospectors** discovered gold at the base of the Rocky Mountains in the summer of that year. The discovery inspired people of all kinds to travel there in search of fortune. Soon, land that was once open to

KNOWLEDGE NUGGET

Denver was settled before Colorado was even a state! In fact, the land belonged to Kansas Territory, which wasn't yet a state, either.

roaming Native American tribes was claimed by people hoping to strike it rich. Some people also purchased land and then resold it to gold seekers. The area was officially a boomtown.

During the gold rush, two towns had formed on either side of the South Platte River—Auraria and St. Charles. In November 1858, a man named William Larimer Jr., claimed St. Charles and renamed it Denver City. The city took its name from James W. Denver. He was the former governor of Kansas Territory. Eventually, Auraria, Denver City, and the surrounding settlements together became known as Denver.

This photograph shows the city of Denver around the year 1898.

Gold was discovered in California in 1849, but few people became rich. The Colorado gold rush may have been their second chance!

This drawing shows three prospectors mining near Leadville.

The Union Pacific Railroad was built to connect the eastern and western United States, but it skipped over Denver at first. When Denver residents heard of this, they raised $300,000 to build a rail line that would meet the Union Pacific in Wyoming. Later, the Kansas Pacific Railroad included Denver as a stop.

Not long after, gold was discovered in a nearby mountain town. Many Denver residents left to chase it, but came back once they discovered how **grueling** the weather in the mountains could be. After returning home, these settlers helped Denver grow into a successful trade center.

Life in Denver must have been challenging for its early residents. In 1863, a fire burned most of the city to the ground. In 1864, a massive flood hit, killing 20 people and causing millions of dollars in damage. Colorado's native people faced great challenges, too. In the late 1860s, Cheyenne and Arapaho Indians were forced out of the territory after they fought back against the white settlers who had taken their land.

The arrival of railroads in the 1870s brought great change to Denver. People were now able to easily travel to and from the city. Silver was discovered in Leadville, Colorado, in the 1880s, and Denver became an exciting boomtown once again. By 1890, its population had reached 106,713.

This photo from the 1890s shows a railroad bridge near Buena Vista, Colorado.

Unfortunately, the excitement didn't last long. The silver market crashed in 1893. Denver's richest residents who had made a fortune on silver were now **penniless**. Many people abandoned the city. Denver rebounded around the turn of the century. Farming, cattle ranching, and tourism helped the city's economy grow strong again.

Denver soon became a food-processing center. "Food processing" means taking foods like meat from cattle ranchers or crops from farmers and getting them ready to ship to

Cattle were herded across Colorado to reach the railroad stop in Denver.

people to eat. New industry created new jobs in Denver. **Immigrants** began to arrive in search of work. Many of the immigrants came from Germany. Others came from other countries around the world. During World War II, the U.S. military established many facilities around Denver. In the 1970s, a rise in oil production brought more changes to the city. Skyscrapers replaced Western-style **saloons** and buildings. By the 1990s, Denver began attracting tourists in search of good weather, beautiful landscapes, and urban fun.

Skyscrapers in modern Denver

CHAPTER 4

The Mile-High City

Today, Denver has many **spectacular** offerings that make it unlike any other place in America. It's called the "Mile-High City" because it's exactly 5,280 feet—one mile—above sea level. It's known for its hot, dry, and sunny climate. In fact, Denver averages about 300 days of sunshine a year.

Many people think Denver is a mountain town, but it actually isn't in the mountains at all! It sits 12 miles (19 km) east of the Rocky Mountains, which provide a beautiful backdrop to all the city's activities. With the mountains so close, residents and visitors have year-round access to hiking, rock climbing, skiing, and snowboarding.

Denver is the capital of Colorado and the 23rd most populated city in the United States. In 2014, the city's population reached 663,862. More than 2.7 million people live in the

EXACTLY A MILE HIGH
The 13th step of the State Capitol Building in downtown Denver measures exactly 5,280 feet (1 mile) above sea level.

The city of Denver covers 155 square miles (401 sq km).

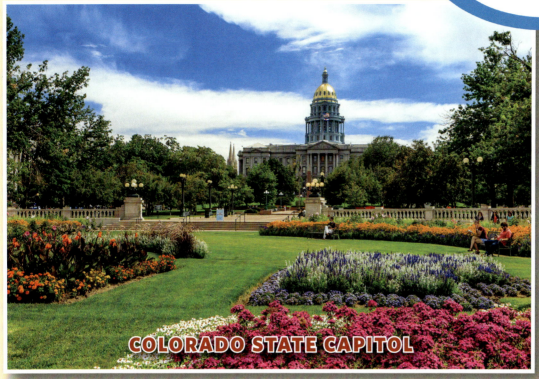

COLORADO STATE CAPITOL

surrounding metro area. Suburbs include Arvada, Lakewood, Broomfield, Westminster, Aurora, and Littleton. Some of Colorado's bigger cities, such as Golden and Boulder, are part of Denver's metropolitan region, too.

Denver is one of the fastest-growing cities in the United States, and it's easy to see why. The city has a strong economy with many job opportunities, natural beauty, and plenty of great weather.

Denver's residents come from many backgrounds. The 2010 U.S. Census recorded the city's population to be 53 percent white, 31 percent Hispanic, and 10 percent African American. The city's Asian and Native American population is less than 5 percent.

CHAPTER 5

Denver vs. Golden

Denver often gets the credit for being Colorado's capital and best-known city. Long ago, however, Golden, Colorado, put up a good fight to claim those titles.

Golden is located about 15 miles (24 km) west of Denver. It was settled around the same time as Denver. Like Denver, Golden was also settled because of the nearby gold discovery in 1858. Golden benefited greatly from its location. As the last "flat place" before the mountains, gold seekers stopped there to load up on the food and supplies they needed before beginning their journey. Golden became so **prosperous** that it was the capital of Colorado Territory from 1862 to 1867. When Colorado became a state in 1876, Colorado's leaders voted to make Denver the state's capital. Residents of Golden were very angry!

The state capital wasn't the only thing the settlements competed over. They competed

CENTRAL HUB

The Colorado Central Railroad was built to be the main railroad junction for all the rail lines that ran into the Rocky Mountains. Railroad workers started building lines to mining communities in the 1870s.

Golden City was named after a miner named Tom Golden.

GOLDEN, COLORADO

over railroads, too. Construction began on the Colorado Central Railroad in Golden in 1868. Around the same time, Denver businessmen formed the Denver Pacific Railway. The two cities raced to connect their railroad to the Union Pacific Railroad in Cheyenne. Whichever Colorado city connected to the railroad first would become the territory's economic center. All the people and goods that came to Colorado would pass through that city. Denver eventually won. This caused the city of Denver to grow and prosper.

COMPETING TO BE #1

Denver won the railroad race because the city's business leaders were able to convince Congress to give them money to build the railroad. The money paid for construction over the South Platte River, which sped up their progress in reaching Cheyenne, Wyoming.

CHAPTER 6

Railroads Bring Change

The railroad race between Denver and Golden says a lot about the importance of railroads in the 1800s. Railroads brought people, money, and trade into new areas. They helped towns grow into cities. They helped new businesses and industries grow and provide plenty of jobs to people in search of work. People from all over the world came to Colorado, including American pioneers, as well as German, Irish, Scotch, and Scandinavian immigrants.

Railroads were **instrumental** to the growth of Colorado's cities. Denver's population and business activity tripled after connecting to the Union Pacific Railroad in 1870. Throughout the 1870s, the territory's population continued to grow. By 1880, Colorado's population was five times what it was at the beginning of the decade.

KNOWLEDGE NUGGET

Railroads made it easier than ever to transport mining products, such as iron ore and coal, crops, and meat from Colorado to other areas of the United States.

More miles of rail were constructed in Colorado during the silver boom of the 1880s than at any other time in the state's history.

In the 1880s, the discovery of silver made railroads an essential part of the state's industry. By then, several rail lines had been built from the towns in the Front Range to silver mines in the mountains. Trains were essential in carrying the tools, supplies, food,

The Durango and Silverton Railroad was opened in 1881 to carry silver from mines in the San Juan Mountains.

materials, and workers to and from the mines into cities such as Golden, Denver, and Boulder. Railroads also carried tourists to and from the cities. Many of them came to Colorado's cities because they were simply interested in where the railroads could take them. The economic and social impact of railroads and their role in the growth of Colorado and its cities are things that can never be overestimated.

FROM SEA TO SHINING SEA

In 1862, the U.S. government decided to fund the building of a railroad that connected both sides of the country. At the time, the American people were interested in the idea of Manifest Destiny. This means trying to expand and settle the United States from coast to coast. By 1869, the project was completed, and it changed America forever.

CHAPTER 7

Boomtowns That Boomed

The discovery of gold and silver, the expansion of railroads, and Americans' strong desire to settle the West made the 19th century one of the most exciting times in history. Colorado needed to accommodate the thousands of people who both settled and passed through the state. Boomtowns sprang up everywhere. These towns brought with them a flurry of activity that sometimes lasted and sometimes didn't.

Denver and Golden are two examples of successful cities that began as boomtowns. After finally becoming accessible by rail, Denver's population increased from 6,829 in 1870 to 38,644 in 1880. The population only increased as time went on. As a gateway to the mountains during the Colorado gold rush, Golden quickly became a center of trade and industry. After a series of population gains and losses, Golden today is home to about 20,000 people.

Colorado's slopes are very popular amongst skiers. The state welcomed 11 million skiers in the 2013–2014 season.

Today, the former boomtown of Breckenridge is a popular ski resort town.

Colorado is known as much for its bustling metropolises as it is for its beautiful ski destinations. Some of the most recognizable ski towns—Aspen, Breckenridge, Crested Butte, and Telluride—were once boomtowns just like Denver and Golden.

KNOWLEDGE NUGGET

Silver Nuggets

The largest piece of silver ever mined was found in the Smuggler mine near Aspen. It weighed 2,350 pounds (1,066 kg)! Believe it or not, it was found one year after the silver market crashed.

The Roaring Fork River near the town of Aspen

Aspen, Colorado, lies near the Roaring Fork River on the western side of the Rocky Mountains. Once home to Ute Indians, prospectors settled Aspen around 1878. They named it for the beautiful trees found there. The location proved fortunate. When silver was discovered in the 1880s, the people of Aspen were close by. The city boomed. By 1891, the small mountain town of just 300 residents now had a population of around 12,000. The city had several newspapers, an opera house,

A WESTERN SALOON
The Gold Pan Saloon opened in Breckenridge in 1859. It's still in operation today! It's the oldest continuously running saloon in the western United States.

two theaters, and a lot of wealth to go around. Aspen was the place to be—but not for long. When the silver market crashed in 1893, Aspen crashed with it. Mines closed, the work dried up, and people left. The mountain town remained quiet until the 1940s, when many cultural institutions and the city's first ski resort opened. These decisions transformed the city. Today, it's a popular—and wealthy—ski destination.

Breckenridge was founded in 1859 when gold was discovered in the nearby Blue River. Breckenridge became a boomtown when prospectors started mining in the mountains in the 1870s. Money generated by the mining industry helped to build schools, bars, restaurants, theaters, and hotels. The mining industry near Breckenridge lasted until the 1940s. When it folded, the town lost much of its population. But after the first ski resort opened in the 1960s, Breckenridge's economy bounced back. Money earned from tourism has turned Breckenridge into a boomtown once again.

Aspen trees are usually found in groups. One tree can spread its roots underground and pop up new trees nearby.

23

Once called "the town that wouldn't die," Crested Butte, Colorado, survived the ups and downs of the mining industry after it was settled in 1880. While other mining places declined, Crested Butte held strong. It was a supply town for other towns in the area. The ranching and farming industries also kept Crested Butte afloat. Today, Crested Butte is sometimes called "Colorado's last true ski town" because it offers spectacular skiing and a rural, small-town feel.

THE TRUE WILD WEST
Bank robber Butch Cassidy brought a band of outlaws to Telluride in 1889. Cassidy and his Wild Bunch stole $24,000 from the San Miguel National Bank.

The first mining claim in what is now Telluride was made in 1875. The mines in this area were rich with zinc, lead, silver, gold, and copper. A mining camp was established in the area in the 1880s. In 1890, the town really boomed because the railroads arrived. Telluride's population grew to 5,000. All the busy parts of a boomtown—including saloons, restaurants, banks, and theaters—grew because of the mining industry. Like other mining towns, Telluride went bust after the crash of silver. It came back to life in the 1970s after its first ski resort opened. Telluride's current population is about half of what it was when it was a boomtown. However, it's home to many popular events and festivals. This includes the famous Telluride Bluegrass Festival. It brings thousands of people to the town every year.

Bluegrass Festival in Telluride

YEAR-ROUND ADVENTURE

Crested Butte is a popular ski destination, but it has plenty of year-round fun for the adventurous. In winter, the mountains offer downhill skiing, backcountry skiing, and snowboarding. In summer, the mountains become a popular place for mountain biking and hiking. It's also the wildflower capital of Colorado!

CHAPTER 8

Boomtowns That Went Bust

Not every boomtown was able to hold on to its success. Many Colorado towns died out as quickly as they sprang to life. Some boomtowns went bust and came close to becoming ghost towns.

St. Elmo ghost town in the Colorado Rocky Mountains

KNOWLEDGE NUGGET

Boo!
A ghost town is a deserted town with empty buildings and no people. Many ghost towns were once boomtowns that formed because of an important economic discovery, but were abandoned when the luck ran out.

Why did silver bust and change the course of all of these towns? In the 19th century, American farmers were experiencing a **depression** that affected the whole country's economy. Many members of the United States government felt that the government could help repair the economy by purchasing silver. There was an increase in the amount of silver because of all that had been discovered in Colorado. Congress passed the Silver Purchase Act in 1890, which called for the purchase

SILVER ORE

of 4.5 million ounces of silver a month. Colorado miners must've been thrilled! However, the increased supply of silver drove prices down—a lot. Silver became almost worthless, sending shockwaves through Colorado's mining industry. Congress repealed, or did away with, the Silver Purchase Act in 1893.

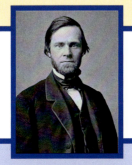

The Silver Purchase Act is officially called the Sherman Silver Purchase Act after John Sherman, a senator who helped get it passed.

CRIPPLE CREEK, COLORADO

Cripple Creek, Colorado, is a tiny town that lies southwest of Pikes Peak. In 2013, its population was estimated to be just 1,169. But in 1901, it was home to more than 50,000 people. Cripple Creek's quick rise and even quicker fall are directly tied to gold.

Prospectors settled near Pikes Peak in 1859. They didn't realize that the riches were contained deep inside the mountains. In 1891, a man named Robert Womack made Cripple Creek's first gold discovery. In the years that

Cripple Creek is home to a number of festivals through the year. One is the Cripple Creek Ice Festival where sculptors come from around the world to carve huge ice sculptures. Another is Donkey Derby Days, which is a weekend full of fun events for the whole family and also includes a donkey race.

followed, more than 22.4 million ounces of gold were mined from the Cripple Creek Mining District. The biggest claim might have been on July 4, 1901. The carpenter William Scott Stratton discovered the Independence gold mine near Cripple Creek. His discovery eventually earned him $37.5 million. He was one of 30 millionaires the boomtown produced.

After 1920, gold production in the United States fell, and Cripple Creek's population fell with it. There were fewer than 1,000 people in Cripple Creek by 1960. Its population remains small today. Visitors to Cripple Creek can tour an authentic gold mine, traveling the same tunnels that once made many people rich.

ALL ABOARD!

If you ever visit Cripple Creek, make sure to get on board the Cripple Creek & Victor Narrow Gauge Railroad. The steam train takes visitors back in time as it explores the historic gold mining district.

A former gold mine in Cripple Creek, Colorado

Leadville is sometimes called the "two-mile-high city" because of how high it sits above sea level. It can also be called a boomtown that went bust. Gold was discovered south of Leadville in 1860, which attracted more than 8,000 prospectors to the place they called "Oro City" ("oro" is Spanish for "gold"). Prospectors, using just **sluices** and pans, uncovered more than $4 million worth of gold in the area.

HORACE TABOR

In 1878, Horace Tabor and two miners found silver in mines near Leadville. This started the city's next boom, which helped Leadville's population rise to 30,000 by 1880. Tabor, now a silver **tycoon** and millionaire, built banks, hotels,

In 2014, the Tabor Opera House got a new owner. The owner hopes to restore the theater to its former glory and reopen it.

and the Tabor Opera House. With saloons, restaurants, stores, and dance halls, Leadville was the place to be. Unfortunately, in 1893, the U.S. government stopped buying silver, and the market crashed. Leadville's economy crashed, too. Over the next century, the once-vibrant mining town experienced more economic downturns and environmental pollution from its former mining days. Today, however, Leadville has cleaned up 98 percent of the pollution. Its efforts to promote tourism and its unique history draw many visitors to the area.

Tiny Creede, Colorado, faced a similar fate to Cripple Creek and Leadville. Anywhere from 6,000 to 10,000 people flooded the town after silver was discovered there in 1890. But they left as quickly as they came. Creede became a near ghost town for many years. There are still signs of the city's past today—storefronts from the 1890s greet modern-day travelers, who visit Creede to fish, hike, raft, and cycle through the San Juan Mountains.

At its height, some of the most famous people of the 19th century performed at the Tabor Opera House, including magician Harry Houdini, musician John Philip Sousa, and writer Oscar Wilde.

CHAPTER 9

The City That Washed Away

RECOVERY AND COMEBACK

Pueblo was nearly lost to history because of the Great Flood. Thanks to the residents' courage, they banded together to help each other and repair the damage. And it's lucky for us they did. Today, Pueblo is a true Colorado destination. The city is known for its great Mexican food and for the special variety of green chilies that are grown there. Pueblo is also home to Colorado's state fair, which visits the city every August. Visitors love Pueblo for its natural beauty, historic charm, and heritage.

The history of Pueblo, Colorado, begins in 1842 when the city was formed as Fort Pueblo. There were once four separate towns in the area—Pueblo, South Pueblo, Central Pueblo, and Bessemer—but they joined together long ago and became the City of Pueblo. These facts may be interesting, but ask any local about Pueblo's history, and they're sure to tell you about the Great Flood of 1921.

Residents of Pueblo, Colorado, woke up on June 3, 1921, to a day like any other. By the afternoon, everything changed. A cloudburst had suddenly appeared over the city, dropping more than 0.5 inches (1.3 cm) of rain in a matter of minutes. Pueblo, which lies where the Arkansas River and Fountain Creek meet, was perfectly positioned for disaster to strike.

Water levels rose quickly as rain pounded Pueblo. What residents didn't know was that 30 miles (48.1 km) north, a **torrential** downpour

A cloudburst is a sudden, violent rainstorm.

This house was destroyed when floodwaters tore through Pueblo City.

was hitting another part of Fountain Creek. Soon, the Arkansas River and Fountain Creek spilled their contents into downtown Pueblo. Within two hours of the cloudburst, the city was under 10 feet (3 m) of water. It's estimated the Great Flood claimed 1,500 lives and caused $20 million worth of property damage. Pueblo was destroyed, but not forever. Residents, volunteers from nearby cities, and the Red Cross worked together to rebuild the city. By 1924, life in Pueblo was back to normal.

CHAPTER 10

The Grandest Grand Junction

Engraving showing the Ute people

Grand Junction is located in Mesa County in western Colorado. It's unlike other Colorado cities in that it wasn't settled as a mining town. That's because the Ute Indian tribe owned the land until 1881. Beginning in 1849, government treaties slowly forced the Utes to give up their land. In 1879, following an Indian uprising, the last of the Utes in the area were removed to a **reservation** in Utah. In 1881, the land was open to white settlement.

Grand Junction officially became a city in 1882. By 1910, it was no longer a small frontier town, but a city with electric streetcars. It had an economy based on agriculture and

ANOTHER KIND OF "GRAND"
Grand Mesa is the world's largest flat-topped mountain, and it's located east of Grand Junction.

A series of mesas provides beautiful scenery around the city of Grand Junction.

businesses, schools, and churches. Grand Junction achieved great growth until the 1930s, when it suffered the effects of the Great Depression. When the American economy rebounded during World War II, Grand Junction's fruit, field crop, and livestock industries boomed. From the 1950s to the 1970s, Grand Junction invested in many manufacturing and oil projects.

Grand Junction is named after the junction of the Colorado and the Gunnison Rivers. These rivers join in the city. But it wasn't always named that. It was first called "Ute," then "West Denver."

OIL DERRICKS

When the oil industry collapsed in the 1980s, Grand Junction suffered, but came back thanks to tourism and new industries. It became the headquarters for uranium production and the transportation hub of the Colorado Plateau. From 1990 to 2000, the population doubled to almost 42,000 people. Today,

GRAND JUNCTION FROM THE AIR

Grand Junction is the closest city to Colorado National Monument. This is a protected park with beautiful canyons and a wide range of wildlife.

DINOSAUR NATIONAL MONUMENT

Grand Junction's population nears 60,000. It's the most populated city on the western side of the state, and the 15th most populated city in Colorado.

Grand Junction is a great place to find dinosaurs—or their bones, at least. The city and the surrounding area are known as the "Dinosaur Diamond," which is an area rich with fossils.

WRANGLE UP SOME FACTS

Remains of the *Stegosaurus* and *Brachiosaurus* have been discovered near Grand Junction.

37

CHAPTER 11

"The All-American City"

The people of the United States come from many walks of life. No two people are the same, and this diversity is something that makes our country great. In 1999, one city was recognized because its population was said to best represent the overall population of the United States. This city is Fountain, Colorado.

According to data gathered by the U.S. Census Bureau, in 1999, Fountain's race and income **statistics** were closest to the same statistics that were measured across the entire country that year. It seemed as though Fountain could be taken as a symbol of the people of the United States, and for that reason, the *New York Times* named it "the Millennium City." In 2002, Fountain received the National Civic League's All-America City Award, which recognizes communities that work together to make their city and the lives of its citizens better.

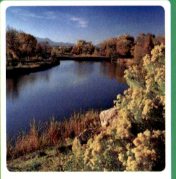

Fountain was named by French explorers, who named it after the nearby Fountain Creek.

Fountain was once a temporary camping spot for Ute, Arapaho, and Cheyenne Indians.

The city of Fountain is celebrated for its diversity.

Fountain isn't just a city of titles—it has plenty of natural beauty, too. Fountain sits at the base of Pikes Peak, and with Colorado Springs just 10 miles (16.1 km) away, residents of and visitors to this small town have access to everything a big city has to offer.

Fountain is home to Pikes Peak International Raceway, a popular attraction. There are plenty of city parks, old-time buildings, and restaurants for visitors to enjoy.

CHAPTER 12

The City at the Foot of the Peak

Colorado Springs is Colorado's second-largest city. Located 60 miles (96.6 km) south of Denver, Colorado Springs sits near the base of Pikes Peak. Measuring in at 14,115 feet (4,302 m), Pikes Peak is the tallest peak in the Front Range of the Rocky Mountains.

PIKES PEAK

"AMERICA THE BEAUTIFUL"

Colorado Springs's beauty has been dazzling people for centuries. In 1893, a woman named Katharine Lee Bates traveled to Colorado Springs on a teaching trip. While there, she and others traveled to the top of Pikes Peak by wagon. The view inspired her to write a poem that she called "America the Beautiful," which was published in 1895. Her words were soon set to music composed by Samuel Ward, and today, it endures as one of the country's best-known patriotic songs.

COLORADO SPRINGS

Before it became Colorado Springs, the land was occupied by Ute, Arapahoe, and Cheyenne Indian tribes. In 1803, the territory became part of the United States under the Louisiana Purchase. Colorado Springs was founded on July 31, 1871. In its first years, it acted as a territorial capital and also a supply town for miners who were starting to arrive in the area in large numbers. In 1890, after gold was discovered in Pikes Peak's Cripple Creek Mining District, Colorado Springs boomed and its population quickly grew to 50,000. Around this time, it was called the "City of Millionaires" after the people who had made their fortune in or nearby the city.

Pikes Peak may be the tallest mountain in the Front Range, but it's not the tallest mountain in Colorado. That honor belongs to Mount Elbert. It reaches 14,440 feet (4,401 m).

41

GARDEN OF THE GODS

Colorado Springs has grown a lot since then. Its main industries are defense, technology, and tourism. It began its strong military ties in the 1940s, when the U.S. Army opened a base called Camp Carson. The United States Air Force Academy came to the area in 1954. In addition to the U.S. Air Force Academy, Colorado Springs is home to Peterson Air Force Base, the U.S. Space Command, and the North American Aerospace Defense Command (NORAD).

The city's technology roots are strong, thanks to international companies such as DISH Network, Clear Channel, and Century Link having a strong presence in the area.

Colorado Springs is a popular destination for tourists in search of beautiful landscapes. Thousands of people pass through each year on their way to see Pikes Peak, but that's just one of the natural features Colorado Springs offers. Garden of the Gods is a public park that features enormous red rock formations. Also in Colorado Springs is Seven Falls, a 181-foot (55 m) waterfall. The hike to the falls is said to be the "grandest mile of scenery in Colorado."

SEVEN FALLS

KNOWLEDGE NUGGET

Go for the Gold!
The United States Olympic Training Center is located in Colorado Springs.

CHAPTER 13

Other Notable Cities

The old-time charm of Fort Collins' Old Town district inspired the design of Disneyland's Main Street USA attraction.

Like most of Colorado's cities, Boulder was settled when gold seekers arrived in the area in 1858. The settlement grew as more people arrived, and the city was connected by rail in 1873. The city's economy struggled around the turn of the century, but money earned through tourism helped keep it afloat. As businesses and new industry succeeded in the area, the population grew, and today it's around 103,000.

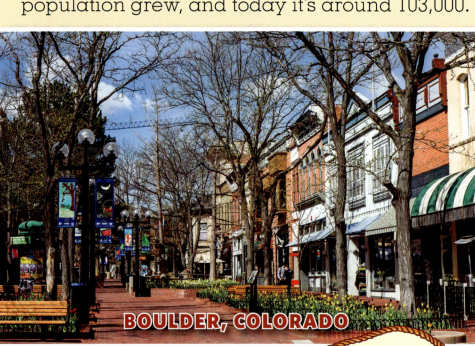

BOULDER, COLORADO

Pearl Street in downtown Boulder has been the city's main shopping district since the late 1800s.

Boulder offers many fun and unique things to do, including outdoor activities, great food, and great shopping. Visitors can tour the Celestial Seasonings tea factory (the largest tea manufacturer in North America) or visit any of the delicious restaurants that caused *Bon Appetit* magazine to name Boulder "America's Foodiest Town" in 2010.

About an hour north of Boulder is the city of Fort Collins, which was once named the best place in the country to live. The city's Old Town neighborhood is a historic district of 23 preserved buildings, which provide a look back at the past. Many people feel Fort Collins is a true mountain town that also offers big city attractions.

Down in the southwest corner of Colorado is Durango. It began as a settlement in the 1860s, but was officially founded in 1880. The city became a popular destination after the San Juan National Forest and Mesa Verde National Park were created in the early 1900s. Today, it's known for its natural beauty and small-town appeal. There are plenty of outdoor activities, restaurants, and historical attractions for everyone to enjoy.

The Durango & Silverton Narrow Gauge Railroad, which began running in 1882, still offers rides today! The experience has been called "one of the top ten most exciting train rides."

Glossary

boomtowns—towns that grow rapidly due to sudden wealth

depression—a long slump in an economy

grueling—very tough and demanding

immigrant—a person who travels to another country to live permanently

instrumental—having to do with helping to achieve a goal or outcome

metropolitan—having to do with a city and its surrounding areas

penniless—broke

prospector—somebody who searches for mineral deposits, such as gold

prosperous—successful

reservation—a piece of land set aside by the U.S. government for Native American tribes to live on

saloon—a public place or bar where someone can buy alcohol

sluice—a sliding gate that's used to control the flow of water

spectacular—beautiful and amazing

statistic—a fact or piece of data

torrential—falling quickly and in large amounts

tycoon—a wealthy, powerful businessperson

unique—special or different

Index